Master the Fundamentals of Brazilian Food

Explore More Than 25 Brazilian Recipes and Treat Yourself to Them

By

Heston Brown

Copyright 2019 Heston Brown

All rights reserved. No part of this Book should be reproduced by any means including but not limited to: digital or mechanical copies, printed copies, scanning or photocopying unless approval is given by the Owner of the Book.

Any suggestions, guidelines or ideas in the Book are purely informative and the Author assumes no responsibility for any burden, loss, or damage caused by a misunderstanding of the information contained therein. The Reader assumes any and all risk when following information contained in the Book.

Thank you so much for buying my book! I want to give you a special gift!

Receive a special gift as a thank you for buying my book. Now you will be able to benefit from free and discounted book offers that are sent directly to your inbox every week.

To subscribe simply fill in the box below with your details and start reaping the rewards! A new deal will arrive every day and reminders will be sent so you never miss out. Fill in the box below to subscribe and get started!

https://heston-brown.getresponsepages.com

Table of Contents

Delicious Brazilian Recipes 7

Recipe 1: Brazilian Style Chicken Pot Pie 8

Recipe 2: Classic Brazilian Hot Dog 14

Recipe 3: Grilled Beef Skirt Smothered in an Onion Marinade 17

Recipe 4: Brazilian Dutch Pie 20

Recipe 5: Authentic Brazilian Style Black Beans 24

Recipe 6: Brazilian Style Chicken Wings 28

Recipe 7: Brazilian Style Fish Stew 31

Recipe 8: Brazilian Chicken Croquettes 35

Recipe 9: Tasty Grilled Chicken Thighs with Brazilian Vinaigrette Salsa 39

Recipe 10: Tasty Black-Eyed Pea Fritters 42

Recipe 11: Brazilian Style Cheese Bread 46

Recipe 12: Brazilian Style One Pot Shrimp Smothered in Coconut Sauce 49

Recipe 13: Brazilian Style Empanadas 53

Recipe 14: Potato and Chorizo Packed Empanadas 57

Recipe 15: Brazilian Style Pudim De Laranja 61

Recipe 16: Grilled White Cheese with Some Oregano Oil ... 64

Recipe 17: Hearty Black Bean and Meat Stew 66

Recipe 18: Toasted Manioc Flour with Scallions and Eggs . 70

Recipe 19: Small Coxinha 73

Recipe 20: Delicious Xuxu and Shrimp Smothered in Chile and Lemon 77

Recipe 21: Chocolate Brigadeiros 80

Recipe 22: Moist Brazilian Coconut Cake 83

Recipe 23: Brazilian Style Coconut Kisses 87

Recipe 24: Healthy Passion Fruit Mousse 90

Recipe 25: Traditional Brazilian Flan 94

About the Author... 97

Author's Afterthoughts.. 99

Delicious Brazilian Recipes

xxxxxxxxxxxxxxxxxxxxxxxxxxxxxxxxxxxxxxxxxx

Recipe 1: Brazilian Style Chicken Pot Pie

Looking for a dish that will feed your entire family? Then this is the perfect dish for you. Mimicking a classic American dish, this is one pot pie dish that is packed full of Authentic Brazilian flavor that I know you are going to fall in love with.

Yield: 10 Servings

Preparation Time: 1 Hour and 25 Minutes

Ingredients for Your Chicken Filling:

- 2 tablespoons of Olive Oil, Extra Virgin Variety
- 2 Onions, Medium in Size and Finely Chopped
- 2 Cloves of Garlic, Minced
- 2 Tomatoes, Fresh and Finely Chopped
- 2 Pounds of Chicken Breasts, Fully Cooked and Finely Shredded
- ½ Cup of Green Olives, Finely Chopped
- 1 Cup of Corn, Optional
- 1 Cup of Green Peas, Fresh and Optional
- 1 Cup of Hearts of Palm, Finely Chopped and Optional
- 1 Cup of Tomato Sauce
- Dash of Hot Sauce
- 2 Cups of Chicken Broth, Homemade Preferable
- 1 Tablespoon of Flour
- 1/3 Cup of Milk, Whole
- ½ Cup of Parsley, Fresh and Roughly Chopped
- Dash of Salt and Pepper, For Taste

Ingredients for Your Crust:

- 5 Cups of Flour, All Purpose Variety
- 1 teaspoon of Salt, For Taste
- 3 Eggs, Yolks Only
- ¼ Cup to ½ Cup of Water, Cold
- 3 Sticks of Butter, Cut into Small Sized Pieces
- 1 Egg, Yolk Only, Lightly Beaten and for Brushing

xxxxxxxxxxxxxxxxxxxxxxxxxxxxxxxxxxxxxxxxxxxx

Instructions to Make Your Filling:

1. The first thing that you will want to do is use a large sized saucepan and place it over medium heat. Add in your oil and once your oil is hot enough add in your onions and garlic. Cook until translucent. This should take at least 2 minutes.

2. Then add in your tomatoes and cook for at least 5 minutes or until soft to the touch. Then add in your chicken, olives, fresh corn, fresh peas, hearts of palm, fresh tomato sauce and your favorite kind of hot sauce. Stir thoroughly to combine.

3. Reduce the heat to low or medium and continue to cook until your filling is thick and creamy in consistency. This should take at least 10 minutes.

4. Add in your freshly chopped parsley and stir again to incorporate. Season with a dash of salt and pepper and set aside for later use.

XXXXXXXXXXXXXXXXXXXXXXXXXXXXXXXXXXXXXXXXXX

Instructions for Your Crust:

1. First add your flour and salt into a large sized bowl. Add in your large egg yolks and stir to combine using a spoon.

2. Add in your butter and work it into your flour using your hands. Add some water slowly and continue to stir until a nice dough begins to form.

3. Once your dough forms, wrap it in some plastic wrap and place into your fridge to chill for the next 20 minutes.

4. After this time preheat your oven to 350 degrees.

5. While your oven is heating up cut 1/3 of your dough away and reserve for later use. Roll out your remaining dough and place into a large sized spring form pan, making sure that your dough covers the side of your pan.

6. Add in your filling. Roll out your reserved dough and place over your filling, sealing both top and bottom pieces together. Cut two slits into the top of your crust and brush with your egg yolk and water mixture.

7. Place into your oven bake for the next 25 to 35 minutes or until golden brown in color. Remove and allow to cool slightly before serving.

Recipe 2: Classic Brazilian Hot Dog

This is a simple Brazilian recipe you can make whenever you are looking for a tasty treat to enjoy. Simple to make and made with authentic Brazilian ingredients, this is one dish that is packed with a Brazilian flavor that you are going to fall in love with.

Yield: 4 Servings

Preparation Time: 45 Minutes

List of Ingredients:

- 2 tablespoons of Olive Oil, Extra Virgin Variety
- ½ teaspoon of Red Pepper Flakes, Crushed
- 1 Onion, Yellow in Color and Finely Diced
- 1 Green Bell Pepper, Finely Diced
- 1 Pound of Sirloin, Ground Variety
- Dash of Salt and Pepper, For Taste
- 2 Cloves of Garlic, Minced
- 1, 15 Ounce Can of Tomatoes, Finely Crushed
- 4 Hot Dogs, Jumbo Variety
- 4 Rolls, Large in Size and Brat Variety
- ¼ Cup of Parmesan Cheese, Freshly Grated
- 1 Cup of Bacon Bits, Crispy Variety
- 1 Cup of Peas, Frozen Variety and Warm
- 1 Cup of Potatoes, Shoestring Variety
- Some Mustard, Yellow Variety and for Drizzling

xxxxxxxxxxxxxxxxxxxxxxxxxxxxxxxxxxxxxxxxxx

Instructions:

1. In a large sized saucepan placed over medium heat, add in your oil. Once your oil is hot enough add in your diced green peppers, onions and crushed red pepper. Stir to combine and cook for at least 8 minutes or until your onions are translucent.

2. Add in your beef and season with a dash of salt and pepper. Cook for the next 8 minutes or until your beef is thoroughly brown in color.

3. Add in your garlic and cook for an additional minute.

4. Add in your tomatoes, hot dogs and at least half a cup of your water. Stir to combine and continue to cook for the next 15 minutes or until your sauce is thick in consistency.

5. Place a hot dog onto each hot dog bun. Add some meat sauce over the top along with a dash of Parmesan cheese, a few bacon bits, some fresh peas, a few potatoes and cover with some mustard. Repeat until all of your hot dogs have been used and serve while still hot.

Recipe 3: Grilled Beef Skirt Smothered in an Onion Marinade

Skirt steak itself is one of the most delicious cuts of meat you can enjoy. For the tastiest results I highly recommend serving this dish with some freshly made Brazilian style cheese bread or healthy vegetables.

Yield: 4 Servings

Preparation Time: 4 Hours and 10 Minutes

Ingredients for Your Onion Marinade:

- ½ of an Onion, Yellow in Color and Chopped Coarsely
- 1 Clove of Garlic, Peeled
- ¼ Cup + 1 Tablespoon of Olive Oil, Extra Virgin Variety
- 1 Tablespoon of Water, Warm

Ingredients for Your Skirt Steak:

- 2 Pound of Skirt Steak, Skin Trimmed
- 1 teaspoon of Salt, For Taste
- ¼ teaspoon of Black Pepper, For Taste
- Some Sea Salt, Smoked Variety and for Taste

xxxxxxxxxxxxxxxxxxxxxxxxxxxxxxxxxxxxxxxxxxxx

Instructions:

1. The first thing that you will want to do is make your onion marinade. To do this place your onions, minced garlic, at least ¼ cup of your oil and your water into a blender. Blend on the highest setting until smooth in consistency.

2. Place your steak into a large sized Ziploc bag and pour your onion marinade into it. Coat on both sides and allow your steak to marinate for the next 4 hours.

3. After this time preheat your grill to medium or high heat. Remove your steak from the marinade and season with a dash of salt and pepper.

4. Place your steak onto your grill and sear on each side for the next 3 minutes. Remove from your grill and allow to rest for the next 2 minutes before serving.

Recipe 4: Brazilian Dutch Pie

Here is yet another great tasting Brazilian style dessert recipe that you are going to fall in love with. Decadent, crunchy and creamy all at the same, this is one dish I know you won't be able to put down.

Yield: 10 Servings

Preparation Time: 5 Hours and 15 Minutes

Ingredients for Your Crust:

- 20 Squares of Graham Crackers, Honey Flavored
- 1 ½ Sticks of Butter, Soft
- 12 Cookies, Chocolate Covered

Ingredients for Your Cream Filling:

- 3 Eggs, Large in Size and Yolks Only
- 1, 14 Ounce Can of Milk, Sweet and Condensed Variety
- 1 Cup of Milk, Whole
- 1, ¼ Ounce Pack of Gelatin, Unflavored Variety
- ½ Cup of Water, Cold
- 1 ½ Cups of Cream, Heavy Variety

Ingredients for Your Chocolate Ganache:

- 1, 12 Ounce Can of Chocolate Chips, Semi Sweet Variety
- 1 Cup of Cream, Heavy Variety

xxxxxxxxxxxxxxxxxxxxxxxxxxxxxxxxxxxxxxxxxxx

Instructions for Your Crust:

1. The first thing that you will want to do is place your graham crackers into a food processor and blend on the highest setting until crumbled. Then transfer your crumbs to a large sized bowl.

2. Add in your butter and use your hands to cut the butter into your mixture completely.

3. Press your crumb mixture into the bottom of a large sized spring form pan. Line your cooked around the edges of your pan, making sure to press them against your crust.

4. Cover with some plastic wrap and place into your fridge to chill for at least one hour.

Directions for Your Cream Filling:

1. First add your egg yolks, condensed milk and whole milk into a large sized saucepan. Set over low to medium heat and bring your mixture to a boil. Cook for at least 10 minutes or until a thick cream begins to form.

2. Add your gelatin mixture to this mixture and stir until fully dissolved. Remove from heat and allow to cool completely.

3. Next whip your heavy cream in a small sized bowl using an electric mixer until firm peaks begin to form. Add in your cream mixture and fold gently until evenly incorporated.

4. Pour this mixture into your spring form pan. Cover with plastic wrap and place into your fridge to chill for the next 3 hours.

Instructions for Your Chocolate Ganache:

1. Use a medium sized saucepan placed over medium heat and add in your heavy cream. Cook for at least 5 minutes or until your cream comes to a boil.

2. Remove from heat and add in your chocolate chips. Stir thoroughly or until your chocolate chips are melted completely. Allow to cool slightly before pouring over your cream pie.

3. Cover with plastic wrap and place into your fridge to harden for at least one hour. After this time serve your pie whenever you are ready.

Recipe 5: Authentic Brazilian Style Black Beans

This is an authentic Brazilian recipe that you are going to fall in love with. Serve these delicious beans with a side of rice or another authentic Brazilian recipe for the tastiest results.

Yield: 8 Servings

Preparation Time: 2 Hours and 45 Minutes

List of Ingredients:

- 2 tablespoons of Olive Oil, Extra Virgin Variety
- 2 Cups of Onions, Finely Chopped
- 2 tablespoons of Garlic, Finely Chopped
- 2 Bay Leaves, Fresh and Dried
- Dash of Salt and Black Pepper, For Taste
- 1 Pound of Sausage, Chorizo Variety and Sliced into Small Sized Pieces
- 1 Pound of Carne Seca, Soaked Overnight and Cut into Small Sized Cubes
- 1 Pound of Spareribs, Baby Variety and Sliced into Individual Ribs
- 1 Pound of Black Beans
- 10 Cups of Water, Warm
- 4 Cups of Kale Greens, Fresh
- 4 Cups of White Rice, Fully Cooked
- Some Hot Sauce, Brazilian Variety
- 1 Orange, Cut into Halves and Fresh

Ingredients for Your Farofa:

- 3 tablespoons of Butter, Soft
- 2 ½ Cups of Flour, Manioc Variety
- Dash of Salt, For Taste

xxxxxxxxxxxxxxxxxxxxxxxxxxxxxxxxxxxxxxxxxxx

Instructions:

1. In a large sized saucepan placed over medium heat add in your oil. Once your oil is hot enough add in your onions and garlic. Then add in your bay leaves and season with a dash of salt and pepper. Cook for at least 5 minutes.

2. Then add in your sausage and cook for at least 4 minutes before adding in your beef, spareribs, black beans and warm water. Bring your mixture to a boil before reducing the heat to low and simmering for the next 2 ½ hours or until tender to the touch.

3. Remove at least ¼ of your beans and mash thoroughly. Return to your pot and season with a dash of salt and pepper.

4. Place your kale greens along with your white rice onto a large sized serving platter. Spoon your mixture over your rice and garnish with your orange slices and hot sauce.

5. Next make your farofa. To do this use a large sized saucepan and place over medium heat. Add in your butter and allow to melt before adding in your flour. Season with a touch of alt. Continue to cook until gold in color. This should take at least 3 to 5 minutes. Remove from heat and pour over your finished dish.

Recipe 6: Brazilian Style Chicken Wings

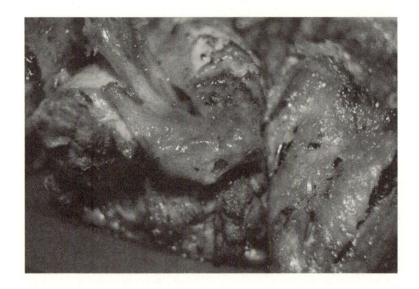

If you are looking for a dish to serve up just in time for the Super Bowl, then this is the perfect dish for you to make. Seasoned with just a touch of lime and garlic and marinated overnight, these wings are not only savory, but they will leave your guests craving form more.

Yield: 4 Servings

Preparation Time: 35 Minutes

List of Ingredients:

- 2 Pounds of Chicken Wings, Small in Size and Bone In
- 3 Limes, Fresh and Juice Only
- 5 Cloves of Garlic, Minced
- 5 Cloves of Garlic, Thinly Sliced
- ¼ Cup of Olive Oil, Extra Virgin Variety
- ½ Cup of Flour, All Purpose Variety
- Dash of Red Pepper Flakes, Optional and Crushed
- Dash of Salt and Black Pepper, For Taste
- Some Parsley, Fresh, Roughly Chopped and for Garnish
- Some Lime Wedges, Fresh and for Garnish
- Some Oil, Vegetable Variety and for Frying

xxxxxxxxxxxxxxxxxxxxxxxxxxxxxxxxxxxxxxxxx

Instructions:

1. Using a large sized bowl add in your fresh lime juice, minced garlic and dash of salt and pepper. Then add in your chicken wings and toss thoroughly to coat in your marinade. Cover with some plastic wrap and place into your fridge to marinate overnight.

2. The next day place some flour into a large sized Ziploc bag and add in your marinated chicken wings. Seal the bag and shake vigorously to coat.

3. Then fill a large sized saucepan with enough oil for frying. Place over medium to high heat. Once your oil is piping hot, reduce the heat to medium and add in your chicken wings. Fry until golden in color. Remove and set onto a plate lined with paper towels to drain.

4. Once your chicken wings are fully cooked place onto a large sized serving dish and add some lime wedges around them.

5. Then use a medium sized saucepan and heat up some oil. Place over medium heat and once your oil is hot enough add in your garlic. Cook for at least 1 to 2 minutes or until golden in color. Pour over your cooked chicken wings.

6. Garnish with some freshly parsley and crushed red pepper flakes if you wish and serve right away.

Recipe 7: Brazilian Style Fish Stew

Here is a delicious stew recipe that you are going to fall in love with if you are a huge fan of seafood. Absolutely savory and packed full of a seafood taste that I know you won't be able to get enough.

Yield: 6 to 8 Servings

Preparation Time: 1 Hour and 10 Minutes

List of Ingredients:

- 2 ½ Pounds of Grouper, Red in Color and Cut into Small Sized Pieces
- 3 tablespoons of Lime Juice, Fresh
- ¼ Cup of Olive Oil, Extra Virgin Variety
- 1 ½ Cups of Onions, Thinly Sliced
- 1 Tablespoon of Garlic, Minced
- 2 tablespoons of Tomato Paste
- 2 Cups of Tomatoes, Roughly Chopped and Sliced into Small Sized Pieces
- ½ Cup of Fish Stock, Homemade Preferable
- 2 teaspoons of Salt, For Taste and Evenly Divided
- ¼ Cup of Piri Piri, Recipe Below
- 1, 14.5 Ounce Can of Milk, Coconut Variety
- 2 tablespoons of Cilantro, Fresh and Roughly Chopped
- Some Rice, Steamed and for Serving

Ingredients for Your Piri Piri:

- 1 Tablespoon + ½ Cup of Olive Oil, Extra Virgin Variety
- 5 Cloves of Garlic, Smashed
- 4 Chile Peppers, Cayenne Variety, Stemmed and Seeds Removed
- ¼ Cup of Lemon Juice, Freshly Squeezed
- ½ teaspoon of Salt, For Taste

xxxxxxxxxxxxxxxxxxxxxxxxxxxxxxxxxxxxxxxxxx

Instructions:

1. Place your fish into a large sized bowl and add in your fresh lime juice. Stir to combine and allow to sit for the next 20 minutes.

2. Next heat up a large sized saucepan placed over medium to high heat. Add in your oil and once your oil is hot enough add in your onions and cook until translucent. This should take at least 3 to 4 minutes.

3. Then add in your garlic and continue to cook for another 30 seconds.

4. Add in your tomato paste, tomatoes, homemade fish stock and dash of salt. Stir to combine and bring this mixture to a boil. Once your mixture is coming to a boil make your piri piri. To do this heat up a large sized sauce pan over medium to high heat. Add in your oil and once your oil is hot enough add in your garlic and peppers. Cook for at least 3 to 4 minutes. Then add in your fresh lemon juice and remove from heat.

5. After this time transfer your piri piri into a blender and season with a dash of salt. Blend on the highest setting until smooth in consistency.

6. Add your piri piri mixture to your fish stew mixture and coconut milk. Stir thoroughly to combine.

7. Once your liquid is boiling add in your sliced tomatoes and cover. Reduce the heat to low and allow your mixture to simmer for the next 10 minutes. Remove the cover and sprinkle your cilantro over the top. Season with a dash of salt and serve your dish with some cooked rice. Enjoy.

Recipe 8: Brazilian Chicken Croquettes

Here is yet another absolutely delicious and mouthwatering Brazilian treat I know you are going to fall in love with. These crunchy balls packed full of wholesome and hearty chicken make for the perfect snack that even the pickiest of eaters will want to enjoy.

Yield: 30 Servings

Preparation Time: 1 Hour and 30 Minutes

Ingredients for Your Filling:

- 1 ½ Pounds of Chicken, Boneless and Skinless Variety
- 2 Onions, Medium in Size and Finely Chopped
- 3 Cloves of Garlic, Finely Chopped
- 1 Tablespoon of Seasoning, Poultry Variety
- ½ Cup of Parsley, Freshly Chopped
- 1 Pack of Cream Cheese, Soft
- 3 tablespoons of Olive Oil, Extra Virgin Variety
- Dash of Salt and Pepper, For Taste

Ingredients for Your Dough:

- 1 Potato, Large in Size
- 2 ½ Cups of Chicken Broth, Homemade Preferable
- 1 Cube of Chicken Bouillon
- 2 tablespoons of Butter, Unsalted Variety and Soft
- 2 ½ Cups of Flour, All Purpose Variety
- Some Breadcrumbs, Italian Style
- Bowl of Water, Almost Frozen
- Some Oil, Vegetable Variety and for Frying

xxxxxxxxxxxxxxxxxxxxxxxxxxxxxxxxxxxxxxxxxx

Instructions:

1. First cook up your chicken and potato in at least 8 cups of water. Add in your chicken bouillon and cook over medium heat until your potato and chicken are both tender to the touch. Remove your chicken and potato. Reserve at least 2 ½ cups of your broth and set aside for later use.

2. Then mash together your potato and reserved broth until smooth in consistency.

3. Place your broth back into your pot and add in your potatoes and butter. Set over medium heat and bring to a boil. Once boiling add in your flour and stir constantly until a thick dough begins to form.

4. Remove your dough and knead for the next couple of minutes or until smooth to the touch.

5. Next make your filling. To do this add in your onions and garlic. Cook over medium heat until translucent. Then add in your cooked chicken, poultry seasoning and fresh parsley. Mix thoroughly until evenly incorporated.

5. Season with a dash of salt and pepper before adding in your cream cheese. Continue to stir until evenly incorporated.

6. Then make your coxinhas. To do this take a piece of your dough and form it into a small sized ball. Flatten it with your hand and make a small hallow indent in the center. Spoon a spoonful of your filling into the middle of your dough and close your dough around the filling, making sure to shape it like a teardrop.

7. Coat your coxinhas with some water and roll in your breadcrumbs. Place onto a large sized baking sheet and continue with your remaining coxinhas.

8. Then fill a large sized saucepan with a generous amount of cooking oil. Heat over medium heat and once your oil is hot enough add in your coxinhas and cook until golden brown in color. Once gold remove and set aside to drain on a plate lined with paper towels.

9. Serve your coxinhas with some hot sauce and enjoy after cooling slightly.

Recipe 9: Tasty Grilled Chicken Thighs with Brazilian Vinaigrette Salsa

If you are looking for a classic and ultimately delicious dish that you can make to impress your friends and family, then this is the perfect dish for you. Absolutely filling and light, this is a great recipe to enjoy without feeling guilty in the process.

Yield: 4 to 6 Servings

Preparation Time: 1 Hour and 48 Minutes

List of Ingredients:

- 8 Gloves of Garlic, Peeled
- 8 Chicken Thighs, Boneless and with Skin On
- 6 Tablespoon of Butter, Fully Melted
- 2 teaspoons of Sea Salt, For Taste
- 1 teaspoon of Bay Leaf, Fresh and Ground

Ingredients for Your Vinaigrette Salsa:

- 1 Cup of Tomato, Peeled, Seeded and Finely Diced
- ½ Cup of Red Bell Pepper, Finely Diced
- ½ Cup of Green Bell Pepper, Finely Diced
- 3 tablespoons of Vinegar, White Wine Variety
- 3 to 4 tablespoons of Olive Oil, Extra Virgin Variety
- Dash of Salt and Black Pepper, For Taste

xxxxxxxxxxxxxxxxxxxxxxxxxxxxxxxxxxxxxxxxxxx

Instructions:

1. The first thing that you will want to do is preheat your grill to low or medium heat.

2. While your grill is heating up place at least one clove of your garlic onto your chicken thighs.

3. Then use a small sized bowl and add in your butter, dash of salt and bay leaf. Mix thoroughly until a paste begins to form.

4. Place your chicken into a large sized pan with the skin side facing down. Place onto your grill for the next 7 minutes. After this time turn your chicken over and baste with your butter paste. Continue to cook for the next 7 minutes.

5. After this time turn over your chicken again and baste again with your butter paste mixture. Remove from your grill and allow to sit for the next 5 minutes.

6. During this time make your salsa. To do this use a medium sized bowl and add in all of your ingredients for your vinaigrette salsa into it and mix well to thoroughly combine. Spoon over your cooked chicken thighs and serve right away.

Recipe 10: Tasty Black-Eyed Pea Fritters

This is another Brazilian style street food that I know you won't be able to get enough of. Typically served during festivals, this is one dish that will become extremely popular in your household.

Yield: 20 Servings

Preparation Time: 20 Minutes

Ingredients for Your Acaraje Fritter:

- 1 Pound of Peas, Black Eyed Variety
- 2 Onions, Large in Size and Finely Diced
- Dash of Salt and Black Pepper, For Taste
- Some Oil, Red Palm Variety and for Frying

Ingredients for Your Filling:

- ½ Quart of Vatapa, For Serving
- Some Hot Sauce, For Serving
- Some Cooked Shrimp, Peeled, Deveined, Fully Cooked and for Serving
- Some Coriander Leaves, Fresh and for Serving

xxxxxxxxxxxxxxxxxxxxxxxxxxxxxxxxxxxxxxxxxx

Instructions:

1. Place your peas into a large sized container and cover with some water. Place into your fridge to soak overnight. The next day drain.

2. Place at least ¼ of your peas into a large sized bowl and cover with some water. Rinse your peas vigorously to remove the skins. Once peeled, drain and place into a food processor.

3. Add your onions, dash of salt and dash of pepper into a food processor. Blend on the highest setting until smooth in consistency. Transfer this mixture into a large sized bowl.

4. Preheat your oven to 250 degrees. While your oven is heating up line a large sized baking tray with some paper towels.

5. Then place some oil into a large sized saucepan and place over medium heat. Once your oil is piping hot reduce the heat to low.

6. Roll your pea and onion mixture into small sized balls and drop into your oil. Fry for the next 6 to 8 minutes or until golden in color. Remove after this time and place onto your baking tray to drain. Set into your oven to keep warm until all of your mixture has been fried.

7. Place all of your serving ingredients onto a large sized serving plate along with your cooked pea mixture and serve whenever you are ready. Enjoy.

Recipe 11: Brazilian Style Cheese Bread

Here is an appetizer dish that you are going to fall in love with. Serve this dish with your main Brazilian course to really bring it together.

Yield: 32 Servings

Preparation Time: 35 Minutes

List of Ingredients:

- 3 Cups of Flour, Tapioca Variety
- 1 Cup of Asiago Cheese, Freshly Grated
- 1 Cup of Milk, Whole
- 1 Cup of Oil, Vegetable Variety
- 1 Tablespoon of Salt, For Taste
- 1 teaspoon of Garlic, Minced
- 3 Eggs, Large in Size and Beaten Lightly

xxxxxxxxxxxxxxxxxxxxxxxxxxxxxxxxxxxxxxxxxx

Instructions:

1. The first thing that you will want to do is preheat your oven to 400 degrees. While your oven is heating up grease a large sized muffin pan with a generous amount of cooking oil.

2. Then using a food processor add in your tapioca flour, cheese, whole milk, oil, dash of salt, minced garlic and large eggs. Process on the highest setting for the next 2 minutes.

3. Place your mixture into each muffin cup.

4. Place into your oven to bake for the next 12 to 14 minutes.

5. After this time remove from your oven and allow to stand for at least 2 minutes before serving.

Recipe 12: Brazilian Style One Pot Shrimp Smothered in Coconut Sauce

Here is yet another delicious and savory Brazilian dish that you are going to fall in love with. It is creamy in texture and is the ultimate soul warming gift for anybody who is a huge fan of shrimp.

Yield: 4 Servings

Preparation Time: 30 Minutes

List of Ingredients:

- 1 ½ Pounds of Shrimp, Jumbo Variety, Deveined, Shelled and Tails Removed
- 5 tablespoons of Oil, Vegetable Variety and Evenly Divided
- 3 Cloves of Garlic, 1 Clove Minced and 2 Cloves Chopped Coarsely
- 1 teaspoon of Salt, For Taste and Evenly Divided
- 1 teaspoon of Black Pepper, Evenly Divided
- ½ of an Onion, Yellow in Color, Peeled and Chopped Coarsely
- 1 Red Bell Pepper, Deseeded and Thinly Sliced
- ½ Cup of Tomatoes, Canned and Finely Diced
- 2 Basil Leaves, Fresh and Dried
- 2 tablespoons of Cilantro, Freshly Chopped
- 1 Cup of Milk, Coconut Variety and Canned
- 1/3 Cup of Chicken Broth, Homemade Preferable
- 2 tablespoons of Lime Juice, Fresh
- 1 teaspoon of Ginger, Ground Variety
- 1 teaspoon of Paprika, Sweet Variety and Optional
- 2 Ounces of Cream Cheese, Soft
- 1 Jalapeno Pepper, Red in Color, Optional and Thinly Sliced

xxx

Instructions:

1. First place your shrimp into a large sized bowl along with your oil, garlic clove, dash of salt and dash of black pepper. Toss thoroughly to coat and allow to marinate for the next 10 minutes.

2. Then heat up some oil in a large sized skillet placed over medium heat. Once your oil is hot enough add in your onions and diced bell peppers. Cook for at least 3 minutes before adding in garlic and cook for an additional minute.

3. Add in your tomatoes, basil and fresh cilantro. Cook for the next 2 minutes before transferring to a blender. Set aside for later use.

4. Add in your remaining oil to your skillet and cook your shrimp for another 2 minutes. Flip and continue to cook for another minute or two. Transfer your shrimp to a serving plate.

5. Add in your coconut milk, homemade broth, fresh lime juice, ginger, dash of paprika and dash of salt and pepper to your blender. Blend on the highest setting or until smooth in consistency.

6. Transfer your blended mixture into a large sized skillet. Bring this mixture to a boil before reducing the heat to low. Allow to cook for the next 5 minutes.

7. Add in your soft cream cheese and stir until fully melted. Add in your shrimp and toss to coat. Remove from heat and transfer to a plate. Serve with a dash of basil leaves, fresh parsley and a few slices of your jalapeno pepper. Serve right away and enjoy.

Recipe 13: Brazilian Style Empanadas

There is no authentic and classic Brazilian recipe quite like this dish. It is incredibly filling and makes for the perfect snack to enjoy any time of the day.

Yield: 20 Servings

Preparation Time: 1 Hour and 15 Minutes

List of Ingredients:

- 3 Cups of Flour, All Purpose Variety
- 1 teaspoon of Salt, For Taste
- ½ teaspoon of Turmeric
- 10 Tablespoon of Butter, Unsalted Variety and Soft
- 6 Tablespoons of Shortening
- 1 Egg, Large in Size and Beaten Lightly
- ½ Cup of Beer, Light Variety
- 1 Onion, Small in Size and Finely Diced
- 2 Tomatoes, Plum Variety and Finely Diced
- 1, 14 Ounce Can of Hearts of Palm, Drain and Finely Diced
- 2 tablespoons of Butter, Soft
- ½ Cup of Sherry, Your Favorite Kind
- 1 Tablespoon of Tomato Paste
- ½ Pound of Shrimp, Peeled, Deveined and Finely Diced
- Dash of Salt and Pepper, For Taste
- 1 Egg, Yolk Only
- Some Oil, For Frying

xxxxxxxxxxxxxxxxxxxxxxxxxxxxxxxxxxxxxxxxxxx

Instructions:

1. Place your flour, dash of salt and turmeric into a large sized bowl. Then cut in your butter and shortening until your mixture forms a cornmeal consistency.

2. Next add in your large egg and beer. Stir thoroughly until evenly mixed together. Cover and allow to rest for the next 15 minutes.

3. While your mixture is sitting add in your onions, tomatoes, hearts of palm and a touch of butter in a large sized saucepan placed over medium heat. Cook for at least 2 to 3 minutes or until soft to the touch.

4. Add in your sherry and deglaze your pan. Then add in your tomato paste and continue to cook for an additional minute before adding in your shrimp. Cook for another 2 minutes. Season this mixture with a dash of salt and pepper.

5. Next add some oil into a large sized pot. Heat over high heat until your oil is piping hot.

6. Roll your dough into even sized balls and flatter with your hands to form a round. Spoon at least 1 to 2 spoonfuls of your filling into the center and fold your dough over your mixture. Brush the edges of your empanadas with some egg yolks. Pinch the edges to seal.

7. Place your empanadas into your hot oil and fry until golden brown in color. This should take at least 4 to 5 minutes. Remove and drain on a plate lined with paper towels before serving.

Recipe 14: Potato and Chorizo Packed Empanadas

Here is another empanada recipe I know you won't be able to help but enjoy. Feel free to add in your favorite kind of ingredients to stuff your empanadas for the tastiest results.

Yield: 12 Servings

Preparation Time: 3 Hours

List of Ingredients:

- ¾ Cup of Chorizo, Finely Chopped and Spanish Variety
- 2 tablespoons of Olive Oil, Extra Virgin Variety
- 2 Onions, Finely Chopped
- 3 Cloves of Garlic, Finely Chopped
- ½ a Green Bell Pepper, Finely Chopped
- ½ a Bay Leaf, Fresh and California Style
- ½ teaspoon of Salt, For Taste
- ¼ teaspoon of Oregano, Dried and Crumbled
- ½ Pound of Potatoes, Yukon Gold Variety
- 1 Egg, Large in Size and Beaten with 1 Tablespoon of Water, Warm
- 12 Empanada Discs, Premade Variety

xxxxxxxxxxxxxxxxxxxxxxxxxxxxxxxxxxxxxxxxxxxxx

Instructions:

1. The first thing that you are going to want to do is make your filling. To do this some oil into a large sized skillet and set over medium heat. Add in your chorizo and cook for the next 4 to 8 minutes or until fully cooked through.

2. Next add in your onions and continue to cook for the next 15 minutes or until gold in color and tender to the touch.

3. Add in your minced garlic, fresh bay leaf, dash of salt, fresh oregano and diced bell peppers. Cook for the next 15 minutes or until tender to the touch.

4. Add your diced potato into your onion mixture and cook over low heat for the next 10 to 12 minutes or until tender to the touch.

5. Add in your chorizo mixture and remove from heat. Stir thoroughly to combine and set aside to cool completely.

6. Next make your empanadas. To do this preheat your oven to 400 degrees. Place your empanada discs onto a large sized baking pan lined with some parchment paper. Scoop at least a spoonful or two of your filling into the center of your empanada dish and fold the dough over, sealing the edges by crimping with a fork.

7. Brush your empanadas with your egg wash and place into your oven to bake for the next 25 minutes or until golden brown in color.

8. Remove from your oven and allow to cool slightly before serving.

Recipe 15: Brazilian Style Pudim De Laranja

Here is a sweet tasting Brazilian dessert dish that I know you are going to fall in love with. It is the perfect dish to make to help satisfy your strongest sweet tooth and please those picky eaters in your household.

Yield: 6 to 8 Servings

Preparation Time: 6 Hours and 20 Minutes

List of Ingredients:

- 1 ¼ Cups of Sugar, Granulated Variety
- 2 tablespoons of Water, Warm
- 2 teaspoons of Lemon Juice, Fresh
- 2, 8 Ounce Cans of Milk, Sweetened and Condensed Variety
- 1 Cup of Milk, Whole
- 1 Cup of Orange Juice, Freshly Squeezed
- 6 Eggs, Large in Size and Beaten Lightly
- 4 teaspoons of Orange, Fresh and Zest Only

xxxxxxxxxxxxxxxxxxxxxxxxxxxxxxxxxxxxxxxxxxx

Instructions:

1. The first thing that you will want to do is preheat your oven to 300 degrees.

2. While your oven is heating up set a large sized saucepan over medium heat. Add in your white sugar, warm water and fresh lemon juice. Allow to warm up without stirring your mixture and cook until your sugar fully melts. This should take at least 5 to 7 minutes.

3. Pour your freshly made caramel into a large sized cake pan and swirl around to cover the bottom and the sides. Allow to cool completely until it hardens.

4. Using a large sized bowl add in your condensed milk, whole milk, fresh orange juice, large eggs and orange zest. Use an electric mixer and beat on the highest setting until thoroughly incorporated. Pour this mixture into your pan.

5. Add some water into a large sized roasting pan and add your cake pan into this roasting pan.

6. Place into your oven to bake for the next 90 minutes or until the center of your cake is fully set and your cake is golden in color. Remove and allow to cool completely.

7. Cover with some plastic wrap and place into your fridge to chill for the next 4 hours. Serve whenever you are ready and enjoy.

Recipe 16: Grilled White Cheese with Some Oregano Oil

These delicious skewers are typically made use a dense white cheese that I know you are going to fall in love with. Make these as a tasty snack or whenever you want to spoil yourself.

Yield: 2 Servings

Preparation Time: 1 ¼ Hours

List of Ingredients:

- ½ Pound of Cheese, Haloumi Variety and Cut into Small Sized Blocks
- 2 tablespoons of Olive Oil, Extra Virgin Variety
- 1 teaspoon of Oregano, Dried and Crumbled
- 6 to 8 Skewers, Wooden Variety

xxxxxxxxxxxxxxxxxxxxxxxxxxxxxxxxxxxxxxxxx

Instructions:

1. Thread your cheese onto metallic skewers and place into some cold water. Allow to soak for at least an hour.

2. Meanwhile add your oil and oregano in a large sized baking dish and stir thoroughly to combine.

3. Preheat your grill to medium or high heat.

4. Drain your cheese skewers and pat dry with a few paper towels. Place onto your grill and grill for the next 3 to 7 minutes.

5. After this time transfer to your oil and oregano mixture, making sure to coat it on all sides. Enjoy while piping hot.

Recipe 17: Hearty Black Bean and Meat Stew

Here is yet another filling and hearty stew recipe that I know you won't be able to resist. While it may seem complicated to make in this recipe, the effort is well worth it in the end.

Yield: 8 Servings

Preparation Time: 3 Hours and 15 Minutes

Ingredients for Your Beans:

- 2 Pounds of Black Beans, Dried
- ¼ Cup of Olive Oil, Extra Virgin Variety
- 1 Onion, Spanish Variety and Finely Chopped
- ¼ Cup of Garlic, Fresh and Finely Chopped
- 4 Bay Leaves, Fresh and Dried
- 12 Cups of Water, Warm
- 2 Ham Hocks, Fresh

Ingredients for Your Adobo:

- ¼ Cup of Cumin, Ground Variety
- ¼ Cup of Coriander, Ground Variety
- ¼ Cup of Salt, For Taste
- 2 tablespoons of Cayenne Pepper, Ground Variety
- 1 Tablespoon of Seasoning, Adobo Variety

Ingredients for Your Meat:

- 2 tablespoons of Olive Oil, Extra Virgin Variety
- 1 Pound of Sausage Links, Breakfast Variety
- 1 Pound of Sausage Links, Smoked Variety
- 1 Pound of Sausage, Chorizo Variety
- 1 Beef Tenderloin, Cut into Small Sized Cubes
- 8 Cups of Rice, White and Hot

xxxxxxxxxxxxxxxxxxxxxxxxxxxxxxxxxxxxxxxxxxx

Instructions:

1. The first thing that you will want to do is make your meat. To do this make your beans by add them into a bowl of water and allow them to soak overnight.

2. After this time heat up some olive oil in a large sized pot placed over medium to high heat. Once your oil is hot enough add in your onions and cook for the next 8 minutes or until translucent.

3. Then make your adobo. To do this use a small sized bowl and add in your ground cumin, coriander, dash of salt, dash of cayenne pepper and adobo seasoning. Stir to thoroughly combine.

4. Add your garlic and dry bay leaves to your onion mixture. Cook for the next minute before add in your beans, your water, ham hocks and half of your adobo seasoning. Bring this mixture to a boil and reduce the heat to low. Allow to simmer for the next 2 hours or until your beans are tender to the touch.

5. After this time remove your ham hocks and shred your meat finely. Add your meat back into your stew and stir to combine.

6. Next use a large sized bowl and add in your sausages along with your remaining adobo seasoning. Toss to combine.

7. Heat up a large sized skillet over high heat. Add in your sausages once your oil is hot enough and cook your sausages are brown in color. Once cooked chop your sausages into small sized pieces and add to your stew.

8. Return your skillet back to high heat add your beef and pork. Cook for the next 8 to 10 minutes for each until brown in color. Add to your stew and allow your stew to simmer for the next 30 minutes.

9. Remove from heat and serve your stew with your hot rice and enjoy.

Recipe 18: Toasted Manioc Flour with Scallions and Eggs

Here is a dish that you can serve up to compliment any other main dish that you may serve up alongside a main dish that you are making. It is so tempting and delicious that you may just want to serve this dish up yourself.

Yield: 4 Servings

Preparation Time: 15 Minutes

List of Ingredients:

- 2 tablespoons of Butter, Unsalted Variety and Soft
- 1 ½ Cups of Flour, Manioc Variety
- 2 tablespoons of Olive Oil, Extra Virgin Variety
- 4 Scallions, White and Green Parts Separated and Sliced Thinly
- 5 Eggs, Large in Size and Beaten Lightly
- Dash of Salt and Black Pepper, For Taste

xxxxxxxxxxxxxxxxxxxxxxxxxxxxxxxxxxxxxxxxxxx

Instructions:

1. First add your butter into a medium sized saucepan placed over low heat. Once your butter is fully melted add in your flour and cook for the next 8 to 10 minutes or until light gold in color. Make sure that you stir constantly as your flour cooks to prevent it from burning. Set aside for later use.

2. Then use a large sized skillet and warm up some oil over medium heat. Once the oil is hot enough add in your scallions and cook until tender to the touch.

3. Next whisk your eggs roughly in a small sized bowl and season with a dash of salt and pepper. Pour over your cooked scallions and scramble lightly until your eggs are set.

4. Add in your toasted flour and stir thoroughly to combine. Season with some more salt and pepper.

5. Slide onto a serving dish and garnish with some more scallions if you wish. Enjoy.

Recipe 19: Small Coxinha

This is a traditional Brazilian style street food is packed with one key ingredient: chicken. In fact the very name of this dish translates to small chicken drumsticks and makes for the perfect snack recipe to enjoy.

Yield: 20 Servings

Preparation Time: 40 Minutes

List of Ingredients:

- 1 Quart of Oil, Vegetable Variety and for Frying
- 3 ½ Cups of Chicken Broth, Low in Sodium
- 1 Onion, Peeled and Cut into Quarters
- 1 Carrot, Fresh, Peeled and Cut into Quarters
- 1 Rib of Celery, Fresh and Cut into Quarters

Ingredients for Your Chicken Filling:

- 1 Chicken Breast, Boneless, Skinless and Large in Size
- 8 Ounces of Cream Cheese, Soft
- 1 Ear of Corn, Kernels Only
- 2 Green Onions, Sliced Thinly
- 1 Clove of Garlic, Minced
- Dash of Salt and Pepper, For Taste
- ½ Tablespoon of Olive Oil, Extra Virgin Variety
- 2 Cups of Flour, All Purpose Variety
- 1 Egg, Large in Size and Beaten
- 1 Tablespoon of Milk, Whole
- 1 Cup of Bread Crumbs, Italian Variety and Plain
- Dash of Salt and Pepper, For Taste

xxxxxxxxxxxxxxxxxxxxxxxxxxxxxxxxxxxxxxxxxx

Instructions:

1. Using a large sized pot add in your oil and set over high heat. Preheat to 350 degrees.

2. Then use another large sized pot and add in your onions, carrots, fresh celery and homemade broth. Bring this mixture to a simmer before reducing the heat to low.

3. Add in your chicken and poach for the next 12 to 15 minutes or until your chicken is fully cooked through. Turn off the heat of your stove and remove your chicken. Allow to rest for the next 10 minutes.

4. Make your filling next. To do this finely shred your chicken using two forks and place into a large sized bowl. Then add in your soft cream cheese, corn, minced garlic and green onions. Season with a dash of salt and pepper and fold thoroughly to combine.

5. Strain at least 1 ½ cups of your poached liquid, while tossing out the rest. Then use a large sized saucepan and place over high heat. Add in your strained liquid and some oil. Bring to a boil before adding in your flour. Stir thoroughly until a soft dough begins to form.

6. Place your dough onto a lightly floured surface and knead for the next 5 minutes or until smooth in consistency. Roll out to at least ¼ inch in thickness. Cut out small sized rounds.

7. Place a spoonful of your filling into the center of each circle. Fold the dough over and pinch the edges together to seal.

8. Then use a small sized bowl and whisk your eggs and milk together until beaten lightly. Place your breadcrumbs into another small sized bowl. Dip each of your pouches into your egg wash first and roll in your breadcrumbs until full coated.

9. Add your pouches into your preheated oil and fry for the next 7 to 9 minutes or until golden brown in color. After this time drain on a plate lined with paper towels and serve while still piping hot.

Recipe 20: Delicious Xuxu and Shrimp Smothered in Chile and Lemon

Here is a healthy and fresh Brazilian style dish that I know you won't be able to get enough of. It's a vivid looking dish that is packed full of a fresh taste that you won't be able to resist.

Yield: 4 to 6 Servings

Preparation Time: 40 Minutes

List of Ingredients:

- 6 Cloves of Garlic, Minced
- ¾ Cup of Onion, White in Color and Finely Chopped
- 2 to 3 tablespoons of Jalapeno, Fresh and Roughly Chopped
- 1/3 Cup of Lemon Juice, Fresh
- 3 Xuxu, Medium in Size
- 1 ½ Pounds of Shrimp, Large in Size, Peeled and Deveined
- ¼ Cup of Olive Oil, Evenly Divided
- 1, 14 Ounce Jar of Hearts of Palm, Rinsed, Dry and Cut into Small Sized Pieces
- 1/3 Cup of Cilantro, Finely Chopped

Instructions:

1. While blending on the highest setting drop your garlic into a food process and chop finely.

2. Then add in your onions, jalapenos, fresh lemon juice and dash of salt. Pulse on the highest setting until chopped finely. Allow to stand for the next 30 minutes.

3. Next peel the skin of your xuxu and slice into thin sized matchsticks.

4. Toss your shrimp with a dash of salt.

5. Heat up some oil in a large sized skillet placed over medium to high heat. Once your oil is hot enough add in your shrimp and cook for the next 3 to 5 minutes or until fully cooked through. Remove and transfer your shrimp onto a large sized plate.

6. Add your xuxu to your skillet and cook for the next 3 minutes or until crispy and tender to the touch.

7. Return your shrimp to your skillet along with your hearts of palm. Cook for at least a minute or two or until piping hot. Remove from heat and add in your processes jalapeno and onion mixture. Stir thorough to combine and remove from heat. Serve while warm and enjoy.

Recipe 21: Chocolate Brigadeiros

If you are a huge fan of chocolate, then this is the perfect decadent chocolate recipe for you to make. These tiny chocolate balls are packed full of chocolatey taste and covered in chocolate sprinkles. I know you are going to love these dessert balls.

Yield: 30 Servings

Preparation Time: 4 Hours and 15 Minutes

List of Ingredients:

- 2, 14 Ounce Cans of Milk, Sweetened and Condensed Variety
- 4 tablespoons of Butter, Unsalted Variety and Soft
- 2 tablespoons of Heavy Cream
- 2 teaspoons of Corn Syrup, Light Variety
- 3 Ounces of Chocolate, Semisweet Variety and Finely Chopped
- 2 teaspoons of Cocoa, Unsweetened Variety and Powdered Variety
- 1 Cup of Chocolate Sprinkles, Your Favorite Kind

xxxxxxxxxxxxxxxxxxxxxxxxxxxxxxxxxxxxxxxxxxx

Instructions:

1. Using a large sized saucepan and add in your milk, soft butter, heavy cream and corn syrup. Next, stir to combine and bring to a boil over medium heat.

2. Once boiling add your chocolate and powdered cocoa into it and whisk well to thoroughly combine. Reduce the heat to low and cook for the next 8 to 10 minutes or until thick in consistency, like the consistency of batter.

3. Slide your mixture into a medium sized bowl and cover with some plastic wrap. Place into your fridge to chill for the next 4 hours.

4. After this time add your sprinkles into a small sized bowl.

5. Then scoop your mixture into small sized teaspoons and roll into balls. Roll your balls through your sprinkles and place onto a baking sheet lined with parchment paper. Repeat until all of your balls have been coated. Serve whenever you are ready.

Recipe 22: Moist Brazilian Coconut Cake

This delicious cake recipe is one that you won't need an excuse for in order to make. For the tastiest results I highly recommend serving a few slices of this cake with a fresh cup of coffee.

Yield: 10 Servings

Preparation Time: 1 Hour

Ingredients for Your Cake:

- 1 ½ Sticks of Butter, Soft
- 2 Cups of Sugar, White in Color
- 4 Eggs, Large in Size and White and Yolks Separated
- 1 teaspoon of Vanilla, Pure
- 2 ½ Cups of Flour, All Purpose Variety
- ½ Cup of Milk, Whole
- 1, 13.5 Ounce Cans of Milk, Coconut Variety
- 1 Tablespoon of Baker's Style Baking Powder
- Dash of Salt, For Taste

Ingredients for Your Sauce:

- 1, 13. 5 Ounce Can of Milk, Coconut Variety
- 1, 14 Ounce Can of Milk, Sweet and Condensed Variety
- 2 Cups of Coconut, Flakes Only

xxxxxxxxxxxxxxxxxxxxxxxxxxxxxxxxxxxxxxxxxxxxx

Instructions:

1. The first thing that you will want to do is preheat our oven to 350 degrees. While your oven is heating up grease a large sized cake pan with a generous amount of cooking spray. Then line it with some parchment paper. Dust with a bit of flour and set aside for later use.

2. Next add in your large egg yolks, white sugar and sticks of butter into a large sized bowl. Use an electric mixer and beat on the highest setting for the next 3 to 5 minutes or until fluffy in texture.

3. Add in your vanilla and beat again to mix.

4. Next use a separate medium sized bowl and add in your flour, baker's style baking powder and dash of salt. Mix until thoroughly combine. Add this mixture into your egg yolk mixture and blend until evenly mixed.

5. Use a separate medium sized bowl and add in your egg whites. Beat on the highest setting with your electric mixer until stiff peaks begin to form. Gently fold into your cake batter until evenly mixed.

6. Pour your prepared batter into your greased and floured caked pan. Place into your oven to bake for the next 45 to 60 minutes or until brown in color.

7. While your cake is baking, make your sauce. To do this add all of your ingredients for your sauce into a large sized bowl and stir well to combine.

8. Remove your cake from your oven and allow to cool slightly. Once cool moisten the bottom of your cake with at least half of your sauce. Poke holes over the surface of your cake and pour your remaining sauce over the top.

9. Sprinkle some of your shredded coconut over the top and place into your fridge to chill for the next 4 hours. Serve after this time and enjoy.

Recipe 23: Brazilian Style Coconut Kisses

This delicious Brazilian dish is one that even the most novice of chefs can cook. It is a recipe that only uses five ingredients and it is also a recipe that can ready in just a few minutes.

Yield: 28 Servings

Preparation Time: 29 Minutes

List of Ingredients:

- 1, 14 Ounce Can of Milk, Coconut Variety and Condensed
- 1 Cup of Coconut Flakes, Sweetened Variety and for Dredging
- 1 Tablespoon of Butter, Soft and Unsalted Butter
- 1 Tablespoon of Vanilla, Pure and Optional
- Some Cloves, For Garnish and Optional

xxxxxxxxxxxxxxxxxxxxxxxxxxxxxxxxxxxxxxxxx

Instructions:

1. The first thing that you will want to do is mix together your coconut flakes, condensed milk and soft butter in a large sized bowl. Stir thoroughly until evenly mixed.

2. Pour your mixture into a medium sized saucepan placed over medium heat. Cook for at least 7 minutes or until your mixture begins to thicken in consistency or until a dough begins to form.

3. Remove from heat and add in your vanilla. Transfer to a generously greased plate. Allow to cool completely.

4. Once your mixture is cool roll into even sized balls and dredge them in your coconut flakes until completely covered.

5. Place your balls into small sized paper bonbon cups. Decorate with your whole cloves right in the center and enjoy whenever you are ready.

Recipe 24: Healthy Passion Fruit Mousse

This is an incredibly easy and delicious South American dessert dish that I know you are going to want to make over and over again. This typical Brazilian mousse dish is made with fresh passion fruit, some whipping cream and sugar, making it the ultimate way to satisfy your sweet tooth cravings.

Yield: 15 to 20 Servings

Preparation Time:

List of Ingredients:

- 2 Envelopes of Gelatin,
- ¼ Cup of Water, Warm
- 1 ½ Cups of Passion Fruit, Concentrated Variety and Unsweetened
- 1 Tablespoon of Lime Juice, Fresh
- 1 + 2/3 Cups of Cream, Heavy Whipping Variety
- 6 Eggs, Large in Size and Whites Only
- 1/3 teaspoons of Cream of Tartar
- 2 Cups of Sugar, White in Color
- 2 to 3 Passion Fruits, Pulp, Seeds and Optional

Ingredients for Your Garnishes:

- 6 Passion Fruits, Pulp Only
- Some Whipped Cream
- Some Passion Fruit, Sorbet Variety

xxxxxxxxxxxxxxxxxxxxxxxxxxxxxxxxxxxxxxxxx

Instructions:

1. Use a large sized saucepan placed over medium heat and add in your passion fruit juice and fresh lime juice. Stir thoroughly to combine and cook for the next couple of minutes or until your sugar fully dissolves. Once dissolved remove from heat and allow to cool completely.

2. Then place your gelatin into your water and stir to mix. Allow to dissolve complete and become soft. This should take at least 5 minutes. Stir into your passion fruit mixture until fully incorporated.

3. Allow your mixture to cool for the next 30 minutes.

4. Next pour your heavy cream into a small sized bowl and beat with an electric mixture on the highest setting until stiff peaks begin to form. Gently fold into your passion fruit mixture until evenly incorporated.

5. Add your egg whites and cream of tartar into a small sized bowl and beat with an electric mixer on the highest setting until stiff peaks begin to form. Add your egg white mixture into your passion fruit mixture and stir thoroughly to combine.

6. Pour your mixture into a dessert mold. Cover with some plastic wrap and place into your fridge to chill for at least 6 to 8 hours.

7. After this time remove from your dessert milk and serve with a topping of some passion fruit pulp on top as well as all of your garnish ingredients.

Recipe 25: Traditional Brazilian Flan

While flan itself may be considered to be a classic Spanish dessert dish, there is no other flan recipe quite like this one. It is easy to make and only requires a few ingredients to put together.

Yield: 8 Servings

Preparation Time: 9 Hours and 30 Minutes

List of Ingredients:

- 1 Cup of Sugar, White in Color
- 1/3 Cup of Water, Warm
- 2, 14 Ounce Cans of Milk, Sweet and Condensed Variety
- 28 Ounces of Milk, Whole
- 4 Eggs, Large in Size
- 1 Tablespoon of Vanilla, Pure

xxxxxxxxxxxxxxxxxxxxxxxxxxxxxxxxxxxxxxxxxxxx

Instructions:

1. The first thing that you will want to do is preheat your oven to 375 degrees.

2. While your oven is heating up use a large sized saucepan and set over medium to high heat. Add in your sugar and cook for at least 10 minutes or until golden brown in color. Make sure that you stir thoroughly as it cooks and allow it to become thick in consistency.

3. Pour this mixture into a small sized cake pan and swirl your pan to make sure it covers the bottom and the sides. Allow your mixture to sit for at least a few minutes or until it hardens.

4. Add in your condensed milk, whole milk, large eggs and pure vanilla into a blender. Blend on the highest setting for the next 2 to 3 minutes or until smooth in consistency. Pour this mixture into your cake pan and cover with some aluminum foil.

5. Next fill up a large sized baking dish with some water and place your flan pan into it.

6. Place into your oven and allow to bake for the next hour and 30 minutes or until the top of your flan is golden in color.

7. Remove from your oven and allow to cool completely. Place into your fridge to chill overnight and serve whenever you are ready.

About the Author

Heston Brown is an accomplished chef and successful e-book author from Palo Alto California. After studying cooking at The New England Culinary Institute, Heston stopped briefly in Chicago where he was offered head chef at some of the city's most prestigious restaurants. Brown decide that he missed the rolling hills and sunny weather of California and moved back to his home state to open up his own catering company and give private cooking classes.

Heston lives in California with his beautiful wife of 18 years and his two daughters who also have aspirations to follow in their father's footsteps and pursue careers in the culinary arts. Brown is well known for his delicious fish and chicken dishes and teaches these recipes as well as many others to his students.

When Heston gave up his successful chef position in Chicago and moved back to California, a friend suggested he use the internet to share his recipes with the world and so he did! To date, Heston Brown has written over 1000 e-books that contain recipes, cooking tips, business strategies for catering companies and a self-help book he wrote from personal experience.

He claims his wife has been his inspiration throughout many of his endeavours and continues to be his partner in business as well as life. His greatest joy is having all three women in his life in the kitchen with him cooking their favourite meal while his favourite jazz music plays in the background.

Author's Afterthoughts

Thank you to all the readers who invested time and money into my book! I cherish every one of you and hope you took the same pleasure in reading it as I did in writing it.

Out of all of the books out there, you chose mine and for that I am truly grateful. It makes the effort worth it when I know my readers are enjoying my work from beginning to end.

Please take a few minutes to write an Amazon review so that others can benefit from your opinions and insight. Your review will help countless other readers make an informed choice

Thank you so much,

Heston Brown

Made in the USA
Coppell, TX
01 November 2021